Moonbeams

William K. Durr
Jean M. LePere
John J. Pikulski
Ruth Patterson Bunyan

Consultant:
Hugh Schoephoerster

HOUGHTON MIFFLIN COMPANY   BOSTON

Atlanta   Dallas   Geneva, Illinois   Hopewell, New Jersey   Palo Alto   Toronto

Acknowledgments

Grateful acknowledgment is given for the contributions of Paul McKee.

For each of the selections listed below, grateful acknowledgment is made for permission to adapt and/or reprint copyrighted material, as follows:

"Clyde Monster," by Robert L. Crowe. Text copyright © 1976 by Robert L. Crowe. Reprinted by permission of the publisher, E. P. Dutton.

"Hideout," from *In the Woods, in the Meadow, in the Sky*, by Aileen Fisher. Copyright © 1965 by Aileen Fisher. Published by Charles Scribner's Sons. Reprinted by permission of the author.

"I Speak," from "I Speak, I Say, I Talk," by Arnold Shapiro. From Vol. 1, *Childcraft — The How and Why Library*. © 1979 World Book-Childcraft International, Inc. Reprinted by permission.

"In the Dark of Night," from *Cricket in a Thicket*, by Aileen Fisher. Copyright © 1963 by Aileen Fisher. Reprinted by permission of Charles Scribner's Sons.

"Keep Off," from *Everybody Has Two Eyes*, by Jean Jaszi. Published by Lothrop, Lee & Shepard in 1956. By permission of the publisher.

"Moon Mouse," adapted by permission of Random House, Inc. from *Moon Mouse*, by Adelaide Holl. Copyright © 1969 by Adelaide Holl.

"Nate the Great," from *Nate the Great*, by Marjorie Weinman Sharmat. Copyright © 1972 by Marjorie Weinman Sharmat. Adapted by permission of Coward, McCann & Geoghegan, Inc.

"A New Teacher," from *Sometimes I Hate School*, by Carol Barkin and Elizabeth James. Copyright © 1975, Raintree Publishers Limited. Reprinted by permission of the publishers.

"Paints," from *I Watch the World Go By*, by Ilo Orleans. Published by Henry Walck, Inc. Reprinted by permission of Friede Orleans Joffe.

"Pippa's Place," adapted from *Here's Pippa Again!*, by Betty Boegehold. Copyright © 1975 by Betty Boegehold. Reprinted by permission of Alfred A. Knopf, Inc.

"Sliding," from *Rhymes About the City*, by Marchette Chute. Copyright 1946 (Macmillan), renewal 1974 by Marchette Chute. Reprinted by permission of the author.

"Talking Time," adaptation of *Quack?* by Mischa Richter. Copyright © 1978 by Mischa Richter. A different version of this story first appeared in the *New Yorker* Magazine. Used by permission of Harper & Row, Publishers, Inc.

"Too Much Noise," from *Too Much Noise*, by Ann McGovern. Copyright © 1967 by Ann McGovern. Reprinted by permission of Houghton Mifflin Company and the author.

(Acknowledgments and Artist Credits are continued on page 222.)

Contents

Moonbeams

MAGAZINE ONE

Contents

Pippa's
Place

by BETTY BOEGEHOLD

"Everyone is too busy to play with me,"
said Pippa Mouse.

"Then," said Mother Mouse,
"you will have to go out
and play by yourself."

Pippa went out to play.
"I know what I'll do," she said.
"I'll find a place to hide."

"It will be a secret place," said Pippa.
"No one will ever find me there.
When my friends want to play with me,
they won't know where I am."

Pippa looked for a hiding place.
She found a hole that was just right
for a little mouse.

Pippa went down into the hole.
Something bumped into her!
"Oh! Who did that?" she called.

"I did!" said Chipmunk.
"This is my house, Pippa.
Who asked you to come into my house?"

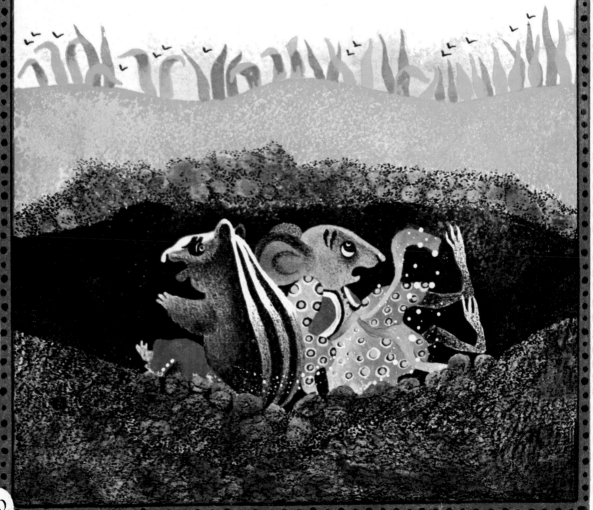

"I thought it was a hiding place,"
said Pippa.

"It is," said Chipmunk.
"My hiding place.
Now go away, Pippa Mouse."

Pippa went on.
She found a good hiding place
between two big rocks.

"I will call this place P.S.H.P. —
Pippa's Secret Hiding Place," she said.
"I will hide here a long time.
My friends will be surprised
when they can't find me."

Pippa went into her secret hiding place.
She sat and waited.
She waited a long, long time.

No one came.
No one called, "Pippa, where are you?"

"My friends can't find me,"
thought Pippa.
"So I will go and find them."

Pippa found her friends playing
by a big tree.

"Hello, Pippa," called Squirrel.

"Come and play with us," said Duck.
"We were busy working, but now
it's time to play."

"Where were you, Pippa?" asked Bird.
"Were you working, too?"

"Yes," said Pippa.
"I was working on a secret.
You can come and see it now."

Pippa took her friends
to her hiding place.
"I call this place P.S.H.P. —
Pippa's Secret Hiding Place," she said.

Everyone went into the hiding place.

"This is a good place," said Duck.

"We can all get in here," said Bird.

"But I thought it was J.F.P. —
Just For Pippa," said Squirrel.

"No, no," said Pippa.
"Now it is E.S.H.P. —
Everyone's Secret Hiding Place!
It is for all of us.
And we can have lunch here
this very day."

Hideout

by AILEEN FISHER

They looked for me
and from my nook
inside the oak
I watched them look.

Through little slits
between the leaves
I saw their looking
legs and sleeves.

They would have looked
all over town
except —
I threw some acorns down.

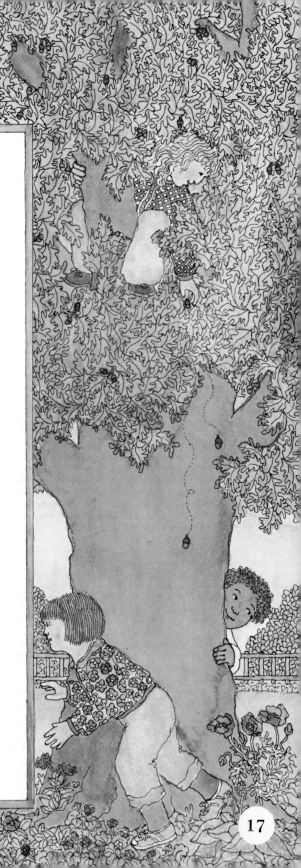

Following Directions

You can make a puppet.

You will need these things.

paper

a paper bag
— not very big

Now read the directions.

Do what they tell you.

1. Make a face on the paper.

2. Cut out the face.

3. Put paste on the back of the face.

4. Paste the face on the end of the bag.

Now put your hand into the bag.
Put your fingers down over the fold.
Make the puppet look as if it's talking.

A New Teacher

by CAROL BARKIN

and ELIZABETH JAMES

My name is Danny.

Mrs. Costa is my teacher.

We do many things in her room

at school.

One day Mrs. Costa said, "I have
to go away for a day or two.

I am going to see my mother.

She needs my help.

While I am away, you will have
a new teacher."

When we came to school the next day,
we saw a man in the room.

"Hello, girls and boys," he said.

"I'll be your teacher while Mrs. Costa
is away.

My name is Mr. Coleman.

Tell me your names."

I didn't want to tell him my name.

Everything in the room looked funny.

All the games and books were put away.
I didn't think I was going to like
this teacher.

Susan and I wanted to play in the back
of the room.
But we couldn't find the things
we wanted to play with.

"Susan," I said, "I think *he* put
our things away."

After a while, it was time to clean up.

Mr. Coleman said, "Linda and Susan
may clean up the paints."

"No!" I shouted.

"Mrs. Costa said Susan and I could do it.
She didn't tell Linda to work with Susan."

I pushed Linda away.
Paint ran all over everything.

Mr. Coleman helped me clean up the paint. He said, "I didn't know you and Susan took care of the paints."

"I wish Mrs. Costa were here," I said.

The next morning, I stopped
at Susan's house to go to school with her.

Susan said, "I hope Mrs. Costa
is back today."

I said, "I hope so, too.
I don't think I like Mr. Coleman."

After story time, Mr. Coleman helped us make popcorn.

That was fun.

And the popcorn was really good!

At play time, Mr. Coleman jumped rope with us.

Then we played some games.

Susan said, "We want Mr. Coleman on our side."

"Now we will learn something new,"
said Mr. Coleman.
"It is a dance.
Keep time with your feet."

Sometimes I bumped into Susan.
Sometimes Susan bumped into me.
We laughed and laughed.
We had a good time.

After school, Mr. Coleman came over to Susan and me.

"I know you can't wait for Mrs. Costa to come back," he said.

"But while she is away, will you help me?

I don't know where to put some of the books and games."

Susan and I said, "We know where they go.

We will help you."

Mrs. Costa came back today!
She asked what we did while she
was away.

"Mr. Coleman helped us make popcorn,"
I said.
"And we learned a new dance."

"Mr. Coleman jumped rope with us, too,"
said Susan.

Mrs. Costa said, "I think you really had fun with Mr. Coleman, didn't you?"

Susan looked at me and I looked at Susan. We *did* like Mr. Coleman after all.

Sliding

by MARCHETTE CHUTE

Down the slide
We ride, we ride.
Round we run, and then
Up we pop
To reach the top.
Down we come again.

What Does It Look Like?

A rock?

Just a rock?

Could it be a cat?

Or a fish?

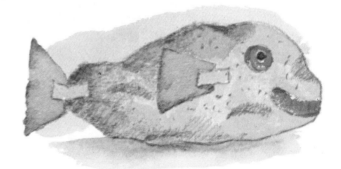

What does the shape of the rock
look like to *you*?

Maybe you thought of a mouse —
or a monster.

Maybe you thought of a dog —
or a frog.

No one will see the shape of the rock
just the same way you do.

Look at the things around you.

You can use them to make things.

What does this make you think of?

A mouse?

A boat?

A turtle?

What does it look like to *you*?

You can make something for yourself.

Or you can make something to give
to someone.

Make something *you* think is fun.

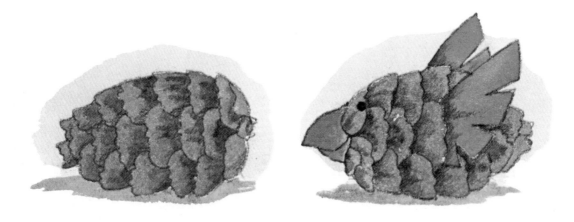

Some of these things will help you.

Laughing Time

1. What time is it when a tiger comes to dinner?

2. What is big and red and eats rocks?

Answers

1. Time to go.

2. A big red rock-eater.

Two Good Friends

by JUDY DELTON

Duck was looking at his clean house.

Just then someone came to the door.

It was Bear.

"Come in," said Duck, "but first
you must clean your feet."
Bear cleaned his feet and went inside.

"Make yourself at home," said Duck.
"Come and sit down."

"Thank you, I will," said Bear.

He sat down in Duck's rocking chair.

Then he put his feet on Duck's table.

"Bear, put your feet on this paper,"
said Duck.

"What do you have to eat?" asked Bear.

"Nothing," said Duck.

"Nothing to eat?" asked Bear.

"Today I cleaned house," said Duck.
"I did not cook."

"Well, I have something," said Bear.
He took two cakes out of his pocket.

"Bear," said Duck, "what are you doing
to my clean floor?

Here, I'll put this paper under your chair."

Bear looked at the paper.
Then he looked at the two cakes.

"Duck," he said, "you are
a very good housekeeper.
But what good is a clean house
if you have nothing to eat?
Here, have a cake."

"Thank you, I will," said Duck.
And he did.

The next day Duck went to Bear's house.

"Duck!" said Bear.

"It's good to see you.

Come on in."

"M-m-m-m," said Duck.

"What smells so good?"

"I am cooking," said Bear.

Duck looked at the two honey cakes sitting on the table.

"Just clean the flour from the chair and sit down," said Bear.

"Bear," said Duck, "I can't sit down.
My feet are stuck to the floor."

"Oh, my," said Bear.
"That's the honey.
Duck, do you want honey cake or pie?"

"I'll take pie," said Duck.

"I've had all the honey I need for one day!"

"OK," said Bear.
Then he cut some pie for Duck and some pie for himself.

"May I have something to eat this pie
with?" asked Duck.

"Today I cooked," said Bear.
"I didn't clean.
There is nothing clean to eat with.
Maybe you can eat with your wings."

"M-m-m-m, that pie was good!" said Duck.
"You're not a very good housekeeper, Bear.
But your pie is the best I've ever eaten."

"Have some more," Bear said.

"Thanks, I will," said Duck.
And he did.

The next day Bear went to Duck's house.

Duck was not at home,

but Bear went inside anyway.

He put some cakes on the table

with a note.

The note said FROM BEAR.

Then Bear went home.

When Bear went inside his house,
he was surprised.

"This can't be my house," he thought.
"My feet are not stuck to the floor.
Everything is clean and put away.
And my table is clean, too."

Then Bear saw a note.

The note said FROM DUCK.

"I must thank Duck," thought Bear.

Just then someone came to the door.

It was Duck.

"Thank you for the cakes," said Duck.

"I was so surprised!"

"And I was surprised, too," said Bear.
"I have never seen my house so clean."

"We really are good friends," said Duck.

"Yes, we are!" said Bear.
"Come in and have something to eat.
But first you must clean your feet."

"I will," said Duck.
And he did.

Books to Enjoy

Where's Al? by Byron Barton

A boy looks for his lost dog
in a big, busy city.
Find out how a cat helps the boy.

Here's Pippa Again! by Betty Boegehold

Read about more adventures of Pippa Mouse.

Gordon's House by Julie Brinckloe

This book has five funny stories
about Gordon, a bear, and his friends.

Two Hoots Play Hide-and-Seek
by Helen Cresswell

A little owl learns a game from some
children — but he plays it in a funny way!

Morris and Boris by Bernard Wiseman

What happens when Boris the Bear tries
to teach Morris the Moose some games?

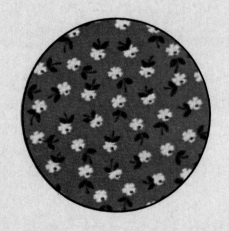

Moonbeams

MAGAZINE TWO

Contents

Nate the Great

by MARJORIE WEINMAN SHARMAT

My name is Nate the Great.
I am a detective.
Let me tell you about my last case.

I had just eaten breakfast.
I had pancakes.
I like pancakes.

Then Annie called me.
Annie is my friend.
She lives down the street.

"I lost a painting," Annie said.
"Can you help me find it?"

"Yes, I can," I said.
"I have found lost pencils, books,
rabbits — even a lost goldfish.
Now I, Nate the Great, will find
a lost painting.
I'll be right over.
Wait right where you are.
DON'T MOVE!"

I put on my detective hat.

I took my notebook and pencil.

I put a note where my mother
could see it.

I always let my mother know
when I am on a case.

Dear Mother,
I will be
back.
I have my
rubbers.
Love - Nate
the Great

I went to Annie's house.
She was eating breakfast.
Pancakes.

"I like pancakes," I said.

It was a good breakfast.

"Tell me about your painting," I said.

"I painted a picture of my dog Fang,"
Annie said.
"I put it on a table in my room.
Then it was gone.
That was last night."

"You should have called me last night,"
I said.
"I like to get on a case right away."

"Tell me," I said.
"Does this house have
any secret hiding places?"

"No," Annie said.

"No secret hiding places?" I said.
"I don't know if I'll like this case.
But let me see your room."

We went to Annie's room.
It had a yellow bed, a yellow chair,
and a yellow table.

I, Nate the Great, was sure
of one thing.
Annie liked yellow.

I looked all over the room.
I looked on the table.
And under the table.
No picture.

I looked on the bed.
And under the bed.
Still no picture.

I looked in the wastebasket.
I found a picture of a dog.

"Is this it?" I asked.

"No," Annie said.
"My picture of Fang is yellow."

"I should have known," I said.
"Now tell me.
Who has seen your picture?"

"My friend Rosamond has seen it,
and my brother Harry — and Fang."

"Let me see Fang," I said.

Annie took me outside.

"Hmm," I said.

"Look at Fang hiding that bone.
He could hide a picture, too."

"Why would he hide a picture?"
Annie asked.

"Maybe it wasn't a good picture
of him," I said.

"I never thought of that," said Annie.

I, Nate the Great, think of everything.

"Tell me," I said.
"Does Fang ever go away from here?"

"Just with me," said Annie.

"I see," I said.
"Then he would hide the picture
right here.
Come."

Annie and I worked a long time.
We found rocks and bones.
But no picture.

At last I, Nate the Great, had something
to say.

"I am hungry."

"Would you like some more pancakes?"
Annie asked.

We sat down to eat pancakes.
The pancakes were cold.
I like cold pancakes.

On with the Case

"Now, on with the case," I said.
"Next we will talk to your friend
Rosamond."

Annie and I went to Rosamond's house.

"I am Nate the Great," I said.
"I am a detective."

"How do I know you are a detective?"
asked Rosamond.
"Find something.
Find my lost cat."

"I am on a big case," I said.

"My lost cat is big," Rosamond said.
"His name is Super Hex.
Here are my other cats — Big Hex,
Little Hex, and Plain Hex."

85

I looked all over Rosamond's house.
There were cat pictures everywhere.

We sat down.
Big Hex jumped up on me.
I did not like Big Hex.
Big Hex did not like me.

"Time to go," I said,

"We just got here," Annie said.

"Time to go," I said.

I got up.

I felt something under my feet.

I looked down.

It was a cat's tail.

"MEOW!"

"Super Hex!" Rosamond shouted.
"You found him!
You *are* a detective."

"Sure," I said.

It was time for Annie and me to go.
But now I didn't want to.
I could smell pancakes cooking.

"Rosamond did not take the picture
of your dog," I said.
"Rosamond just likes cats —
and pancakes.
Now where is your brother Harry?"

Harry was in his room.
He had really painted!
There were pictures of a bird, a house,
and a tree.
There was a picture of a monster.
The monster had three heads.

"Harry does very good work," I said.

"But where is my picture?"
Annie asked.

Where *was* the picture of Fang?
I could not find it.
Fang did not have it.
Rosamond did not have it.
Harry did not have it.
Or did he?

Then a thought came to me.

I said, "I, Nate the Great, have found your picture."

"You have?" Annie said.
"Where?"

"Look!" I said.
"Harry has pictures of a bird, a house, a tree, and a monster with three heads."

"So what?" Annie said.

"Take a good look," I said.
"The picture of the bird is red.
The picture of the house is red.
The picture of the tree is red.
But the picture of the monster is orange."

"So what?" said Annie.
"Orange is great for a monster."

"But Harry paints with *red*," I said.
"Everything is red but the monster.
I, Nate the Great, will tell you why.
Harry painted a red monster
over the yellow picture of your dog.
The yellow paint was still wet.
Yellow and red make orange.
That is why the monster is orange."

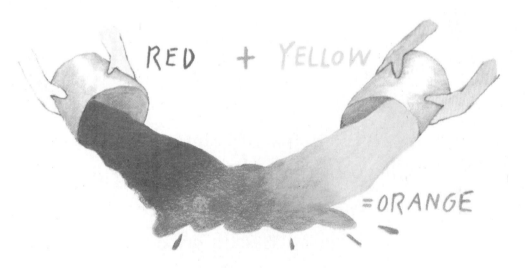

RED + YELLOW

=ORANGE

Annie looked very surprised.
She did not say a word.

I said, "See!
The monster has three heads.
Two of the heads were your dog's ears.
The other head was the tail.
Yes, Harry *does* do good work."

"This case is over," I said.
"I must go."

"I don't know how to thank you,"
Annie said.

"I do," I said.
"Are there any more pancakes?"

I don't like to eat on a case.
But the case was over.

We sat at the table.
Annie and I.
And Harry.

Annie said, "I will paint a new picture.
Will you come back to see it?"

"If Harry doesn't see it first,"
I laughed.

It was time to go.
I said good-by to Annie and Harry
and Fang.
I headed for home.
Rain was coming down.
It was a good thing I had my rubbers.

Paints

by ILO ORLEANS

When I put YELLOW
Paint on RED,
The colors change
To ORANGE instead.

Another trick
That I have seen —
YELLOW and BLUE
Turn into GREEN.

There's magic when
My colors mix.
It's fun to watch them
Doing tricks.

The Scared Little Rabbit

Players: **Storyteller**   **Sister Rabbit**

                Little Rabbit   **Tiger**

                Brother Rabbit   **Fox**

                          Wise Old Lion

Storyteller: Long ago there was
a little rabbit who was scared
of everything.

One morning while she was sitting
under a tree, she looked up at the sky.

Little Rabbit: I'm scared the sky will fall.
What if the sky should fall in right now?
What would happen to me?

Storyteller: Just about that time, something went *ker-plop*!
It was just a small noise.
But it scared Little Rabbit.

Little Rabbit: Oh, my! The sky *is* falling in!
I have to get out of here!

Storyteller: Little Rabbit ran away fast.
Soon she saw Brother Rabbit.

Brother Rabbit: Stop, Little Rabbit! Where are you going?

Little Rabbit: Oh, I can't stop! I don't have time to talk now. I have to get away from here! The sky is falling in!

Brother Rabbit: The sky is falling in? I see no signs of the sky falling in.

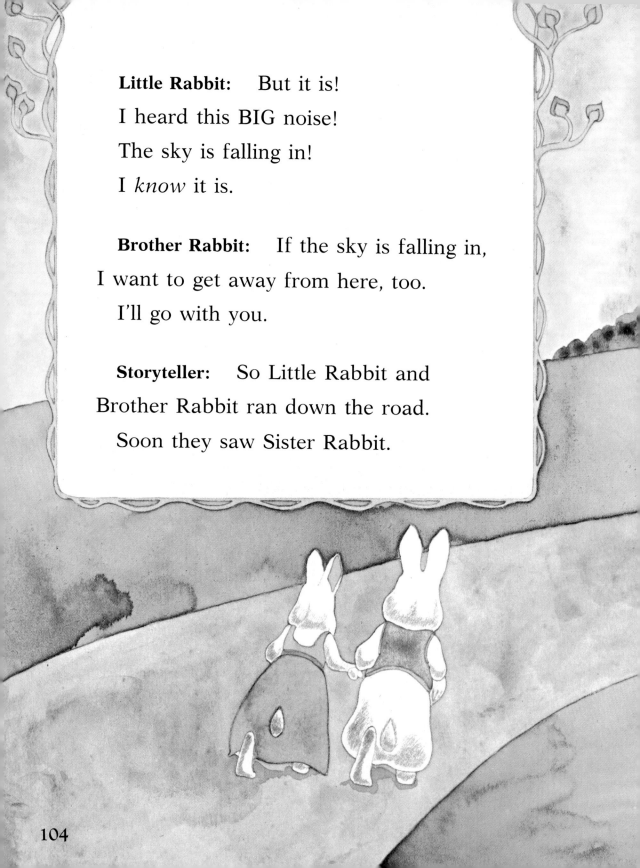

Little Rabbit: But it is!
I heard this BIG noise!
The sky is falling in!
I *know* it is.

Brother Rabbit: If the sky is falling in,
I want to get away from here, too.
I'll go with you.

Storyteller: So Little Rabbit and
Brother Rabbit ran down the road.
Soon they saw Sister Rabbit.

Sister Rabbit: Stop, Little Rabbit and Brother Rabbit!
Where are you going?

Brother Rabbit: Oh, we can't stop!
We don't have time.
We have to get away from here!
The sky is falling in!

Sister Rabbit: The sky is falling in?
I see no signs of the sky falling in.

Brother Rabbit and Little Rabbit: But there was this BIG noise.

We *know* that the sky is falling in!

Sister Rabbit: If the sky is falling in, I want to get away from here, too.

I'll go with you.

Storyteller: So Little Rabbit, Brother Rabbit, and Sister Rabbit ran down the road together.

Soon they saw Tiger.

Tiger: Stop, everyone!
Where are you going?

Sister Rabbit: Oh, we can't stop!
We don't have time.
We have to get away from here!
The sky is falling in!

Tiger: The sky is falling in?
I see no signs of the sky falling in.

All: But there was this BIG noise.
We *know* that the sky is falling in!

Tiger: If the sky is falling in,
I want to get away from here, too!
I'll go with you.

Storyteller: So Little Rabbit,
Brother Rabbit, Sister Rabbit, and Tiger
ran down the road together.
Soon they saw Fox.

Fox: Stop, everyone!
Where are you going?

Tiger: Oh, we can't stop!
We don't have time.
We must get away from here!
The sky is falling in!

Fox: The sky is falling in?
I see no signs of the sky falling in.

All: But there was this BIG noise.
We *know* that the sky is falling in!

Fox: If the sky is falling in, I want to get away from here, too.
I'll go with you.

Storyteller: So Little Rabbit, Brother Rabbit, Sister Rabbit, Tiger, and Fox ran down the road together. Soon they saw Wise Old Lion.

Wise Old Lion: Stop, everyone!
Where are you going?

Fox: Oh, we can't stop!
We don't have time.
We must get away from here!
The sky is falling in!

Wise Old Lion: The sky is falling in?
I see no signs of the sky falling in.

All: But there was this BIG noise.
We *know* that the sky is falling in!

111

Wise Old Lion: Tell me, Fox, where did you hear this BIG noise?

Fox: Come to think of it, Tiger told me about the BIG noise.

Wise Old Lion: Tiger, where did you hear this BIG noise?

Tiger: Come to think of it, Sister Rabbit told me about the BIG noise.

Wise Old Lion: Sister Rabbit, where did you hear this BIG noise?

Sister Rabbit: Come to think of it, Brother Rabbit told me about the BIG noise.

Wise Old Lion: Brother Rabbit, where did you hear this BIG noise?

Brother Rabbit: Come to think of it, Little Rabbit told me about the BIG noise.

All: That's right!
It was Little Rabbit.
Little Rabbit heard the BIG noise.

Wise Old Lion: Little Rabbit, where did you hear this BIG noise?

Little Rabbit: It was by the big tree.

Wise Old Lion: Come and show me the big tree, Little Rabbit.
The others can wait here.

Storyteller: So Wise Old Lion and Little Rabbit went to see the tree.
The others waited.

Little Rabbit: There's the tree.
That's where I heard the BIG noise!

Wise Old Lion: Come over to the tree
with me, Little Rabbit.
I want to show you what made the noise.

Little Rabbit: Over to the tree?
No, not me!
I would not go near that tree for anything!
I am too scared!

Wise Old Lion: Don't be scared.
I'm right here.

Storyteller: Then Wise Old Lion and
Little Rabbit went over to the tree.
Wise Old Lion shook the tree.
An apple came down — *ker-plop*!

Wise Old Lion: Is that the noise you heard?

Little Rabbit: Yes, that's it!
I see now — it was just an apple!
So the sky is not falling in after all.

Wise Old Lion: Let's go back and tell the others.

Storyteller: So Little Rabbit and Wise Old Lion went back to where the others were waiting.

Little Rabbit: I was wrong, friends. The sky is *not* falling in.

Fox: Little Rabbit says the sky is not falling in.

Tiger: Fox says the sky is not falling in.

Sister Rabbit: Tiger says the sky is not falling in.

Brother Rabbit: Sister Rabbit says the sky is not falling in.

119

All: Hooray! Hooray!
The sky is not falling in.

Storyteller: Then they all went home.
There was nothing to be scared of anymore.

Which Way?

Find the best road from Squirrel's house
to Mouse's house.

It is the road with all these things on it.

a red duck

an orange bear

a yellow rabbit

MOUSE'S HOUSE

SQUIRREL'S HOUSE

More Than One Meaning

You know that a word can have
more than one meaning.

The other words in a sentence will help
you decide the best meaning of the word.

Look at this picture.
Then read the sentences.

1. How long has Bob had a **cold?**
2. Sam likes to play outside on **cold** days.

Which sentence tells about the picture?

Look at each picture.

Which sentence tells about each picture?

1. Pig and Duck were hiding by a **rock.**
2. Pig said, "Duck, don't **rock** the boat."

1. I painted the table **orange.**
2. I had an **orange** for lunch.

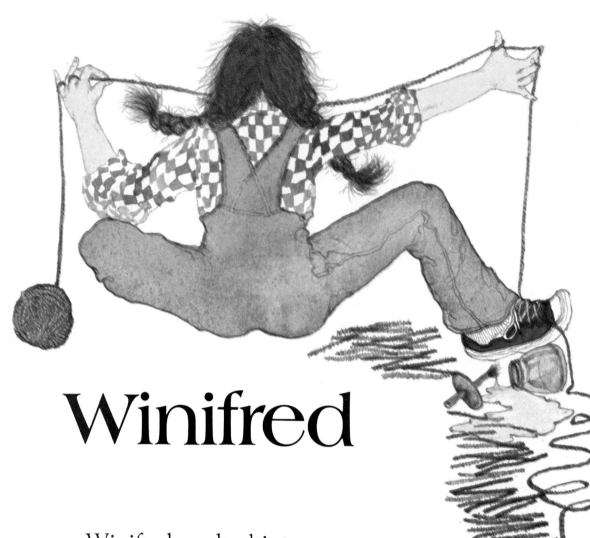

Winifred

Winifred made things.
She made old things and new things.
She made big things and little things.
But Winifred had a problem.
She made things so fast that they were
never very good.

Winifred always gave the things she made
to her friends.

Her friends said, "Thank you.
Thank you, Winifred."

But they didn't know what to do
with the things she gave them.

One day the woman next door said,
"Winifred, I know you like to make things.
Why don't you make things we can use?
Why don't you make signs?"

"Signs," said Winifred.
"What a good idea!"

The next time Winifred went for a ride,
she read all the signs she saw.

When Winifred got home,
she sat right down and went to work.

She made signs just like the ones
she had seen.

But no one could use the signs.
No one wanted them at all.
So Winifred put the signs
all over the outside of her house.
People stopped to look at the signs
on Winifred's house.

People came to the door night and day.
"Are the things on those signs
for sale?" they asked.

"Oh, no!" said Winifred.
"I don't have anything for sale.
Those are just signs."

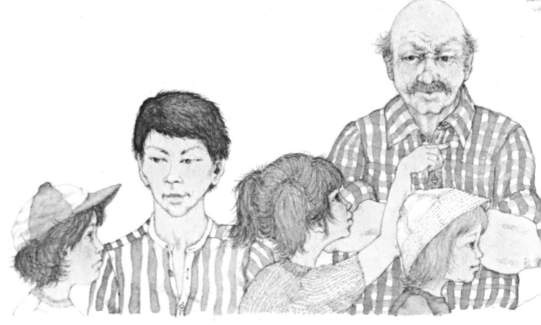

129

Everyone shouted at Winifred.
"Take those signs down!" they said.
So Winifred took down the signs.

But that was not the end of it.
Every time Winifred saw a sign,
she still had to make one like it.

One day Winifred went to the zoo.

When she got home, she sat right down
and made signs.

No one wanted those signs either.

So Winifred put the signs here and
there, up and down the street.

There were red, yellow, gold,
and orange signs everywhere.

The next morning Winifred could hear noises coming from the street.

She looked out.

There were people everywhere.

Everyone had read Winifred's signs.

The people thought lions and tigers had run away from the zoo.

SNAKES THIS WAY

TIGERS

MONKEY HOUSE

TICKETS FOR SALE HERE!

Winifred wanted to run.
Winifred wanted to hide.
Winifred wanted to fly away.
But she didn't.

She shouted to the people, "Wait,
wait, wait!"

Then she ran outside and called,
"I am sorry.
I am so sorry, everyone.
I didn't mean to scare you."

After the people had gone, Winifred
went back into her house.

She made a great big sign.

A friend helped Winifred put up
her new sign.

After that, Winifred was busier
than ever.

The first sign Winifred made was
for Bill's tree house.

Then Winifred made a sign
for the house down the street.

Next, she made a sign
for a good friend.

And one day, Winifred made
a very small sign.

It was for the woman next door
to put on her cat's bed.

People still say, "Thank you.
Thank you, Winifred."
And they really mean it.
Now they know what to do
with the things Winifred makes.

Signs and
More Signs!

A sign is a fast way of saying something.

Some signs have words.

Some signs have words and pictures.

Many signs are just pictures.

Picture signs are used in many places because everyone knows what they mean.

Talk about what these signs mean.

Signs are fun to think about.

This means **Go Fast.**   What does this mean?

This means **Go Up.**   What does this mean?

This means **Go Right.**   What does this mean?

Sometimes signs are put together
to make new ones.

This sign means

Dogs Can Come Here.

This sign means

No.

What do you think this sign means?

You see signs almost everywhere you go.

Signs can help you.

Can you think of a sign that helped you?

Keep Off

by JEAN JASZI

Bird,
Keep off the grass.
Don't you see the sign?
It says, PLEASE.

KEEP OFF
PLEASE

Clyde Monster

by ROBERT L. CROWE

Clyde wasn't very old.

But he was ugly.

And he was growing uglier every day.

He lived in a forest with his mother
and his father.

Father Monster was a big, big monster.

He was very ugly, which was good.

Mother Monster was even uglier,
which was better.

Monsters make fun of pretty monsters.

All in all, Clyde and his mother
and his father were lovely monsters —
as monsters go.

145

All day Clyde played in the forest
doing monster things, like making big holes
and bumping into things.

At night Clyde should have gone
to his cave to sleep.

But he would not go to his cave.

"Why?" asked his mother.
"Why won't you go to your cave?"

"Because I'm scared of the dark,"
said Clyde.

"Scared?" asked his father.
"What are you scared of?"

"People," said Clyde.
"I'm scared there are people in the cave who will get me."

"That's silly," said his father.

"Come, I'll show you.

First, I'll light up the cave.

There.

Did you see any people?"

"No," said Clyde.

"But they may be hiding under a rock.

They will jump out and get me

after I'm asleep."

"That is silly," said his mother.
"There are no people here.
Even if there were, they wouldn't get you."

"They wouldn't?" asked Clyde.

"No," said his mother.
"Would you ever hide in the dark?
Would you hide under a bed to scare
a boy or a girl?"

"No!" said Clyde.
"I would never do a thing like that!"

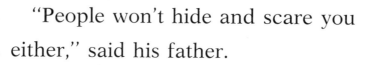

"People won't hide and scare you either," said his father.

"A long time ago, monsters and people made a deal.

Monsters don't scare people — and people don't scare monsters."

"Are you sure?" Clyde asked.

"Very sure," said his mother.
"Do you know of any monsters that were
ever scared by people?"

"No," said Clyde.

"Do you know of any people who were
ever scared by monsters?" she asked.

"No," Clyde said.

"There!" said his mother.
"Now it's time for bed."

"And," said his father, "I don't want to hear any more about being scared by people."

"OK," said Clyde as he went into the cave.

"But could you leave the rock open just a little?"

Books to Enjoy

Hattie Rabbit by Dick Gackenbach
   Hattie is a funny little rabbit,
but she always uses her head.

Henrietta, the Early Bird by Syd Hoff
   Find out why all the animals want
Henrietta the hen to go back to bed.

What Was That? by Geda Mathews
   What is making the night noises
that are scaring the little bears?

Great Day for Up by Dr. Seuss
   Do you like to get up in the morning?
   It's fun when Dr. Seuss tells you how.

Nate the Great Goes Undercover
by Marjorie Weinman Sharmat
   Nate the detective is on another case.

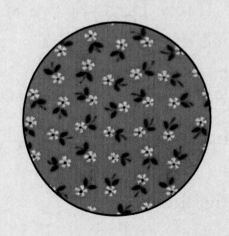

Moonbeams

MAGAZINE THREE

Contents

Too Much Noise

by ANN McGOVERN

A long time ago there was an old man.

His name was Peter, and he lived

in an old, old house.

The bed creaked.
The floor squeaked.

Outside, the wind went *swish, swish.*
Inside, the kettle went *hiss, hiss.*

"Too noisy," said Peter.

Peter went to see the wise man.

"What can I do?" Peter asked
the wise man.

"My house makes too much noise.

My bed creaks.

My floor squeaks.

The wind goes *swish, swish*.

And the kettle goes *hiss, hiss*."

"I can help you," the wise man said.
"I know what you can do."

"What?" said Peter.

"Get a cow," said the wise man.

"What good is a cow?" said Peter.
But Peter got a cow anyhow.

The cow said, "Moo. Moo."
The bed creaked.
The floor squeaked.
Outside, the wind went *swish, swish.*
Inside, the kettle went *hiss, hiss.*

"Too noisy," said Peter.
And he went back to the wise man.

"Get a donkey," said the wise man.

"What good is a donkey?" said Peter.
But Peter got a donkey anyhow.

The donkey said, "Hee-Haw."
The cow said, "Moo. Moo."
The bed creaked.
The floor squeaked.
Outside, the wind went *swish, swish.*
Inside, the kettle went *hiss, hiss.*

"Still too noisy," said Peter.
And he went back to the wise man.

"Get a sheep," said the wise man.

"What good is a sheep?" said Peter.
But Peter got a sheep anyhow.

The sheep said, "Baa. Baa."
The donkey said, "Hee-Haw."
The cow said, "Moo. Moo."
The bed creaked.
The floor squeaked.
Outside, the wind went *swish, swish.*
Inside, the kettle went *hiss, hiss.*

"Too noisy," said Peter.
And he went back to the wise man.

"Get a hen," said the wise man.

"What good is a hen?" said Peter.
But Peter got a hen anyhow.

The hen said, "Cluck. Cluck."

The sheep said, "Baa. Baa."

The donkey said, "Hee-Haw."

The cow said, "Moo. Moo."

The bed creaked.

The floor squeaked.

Outside, the wind went *swish, swish.*

Inside, the kettle went *hiss, hiss.*

"Too noisy," said Peter.

And he went back to the wise man.

"Get a dog," the wise man said.
"And get a cat too."

"What good is a dog?" said Peter.
"Or a cat?"
But Peter got a dog and a cat anyhow.

The dog said, "Woof. Woof."

The cat said, "Meow. Meow."

The hen said, "Cluck. Cluck."

The sheep said, "Baa. Baa."

The donkey said, "Hee-Haw."

The cow said, "Moo. Moo."

The bed creaked.

The floor squeaked.

Outside, the wind went *swish, swish*.

Inside, the kettle went *hiss, hiss*.

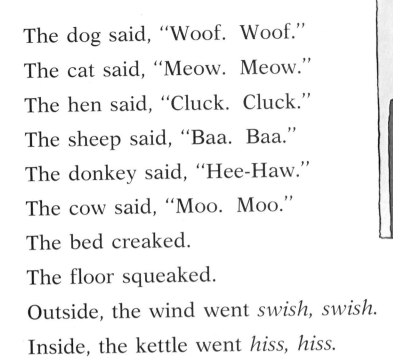

"This is just too much noise,"
said Peter.

So he went back to the wise man.

"I *told* you my house was too noisy,"
he said.

"I told you my bed creaks.
My floor squeaks.
The wind goes *swish, swish*.
And the kettle goes *hiss, hiss*.

You told me to get a cow.
All day the cow goes moo, moo.

You told me to get a donkey.
All day the donkey goes hee-haw.

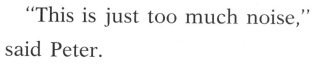

You told me to get a sheep.
All day the sheep goes baa, baa.

You told me to get a hen.
All day the hen goes cluck, cluck.

You told me to get a dog.
And a cat.
All day the dog goes woof, woof.
All day the cat goes meow, meow.

I am going crazy," said Peter.

The wise man said, "Do what I tell you.

Let the cow go.

Let the donkey go.

Let the sheep go.

Let the hen go.

Let the dog go.

Let the cat go."

So Peter let the cow go.

He let the donkey go.

He let the sheep go.

He let the hen go.

He let the dog go.

He let the cat go.

Now no cow said, "Moo. Moo."

No donkey said, "Hee-Haw."

No sheep said, "Baa. Baa."

No hen said, "Cluck. Cluck."

No dog said, "Woof. Woof."

No cat said, "Meow. Meow."

The bed creaked.

"What a quiet noise," said Peter.

The floor squeaked.

"What a quiet noise," said Peter.

Outside, the wind went *swish, swish.*
Inside, the kettle went *hiss, hiss.*

"How quiet my house is," said Peter.

And Peter got into his bed and went
to sleep and dreamed a very

                    quiet

                            dream.

I Speak

by ARNOLD SHAPIRO

Cats purr.

Lions roar.

Owls hoot.

Bears snore.

Crickets creak.

Mice squeak.

Sheep baa.

But I SPEAK!

Lines from "I Speak, I Say, I Talk" by Arnold Shapiro.
From Vol. 1, *Childcraft — The How and Why Library*.
© 1979 World Book-Childcraft International, Inc.

179

The Vowels *o* and *u*

The vowels **o** and **u** can each stand for more than one sound.

Say these words.

Listen for the vowel sound.

stop   got   not

The vowel sound you hear is the short **o** sound.

Find the words that have the short **o** sound.

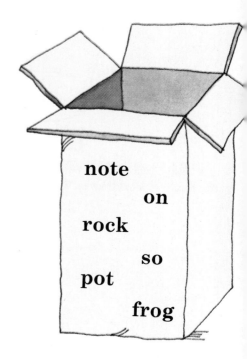

note

on

rock

so

pot

frog

gold   go

box

hole   no

Say these words.

Listen for the vowel sound.

those   cold   home

The vowel sound you hear is the long **o** sound.

Find the words that have the long **o** sound.

180

Say these words.

Listen for the vowel sound.

cut   run   up

The vowel sound you hear is
the short **u** sound.

Find the words that have
the short **u** sound.

but   fun   use

duck

Now say the word **use** to yourself.

The vowel sound you hear in **use**
is the long **u** sound.

Say the names of these pictures.

Find the ones with names that have
the long **u** sound.

181

What Mary Jo Shared

by JANICE MAY UDRY

When it was Sharing Time at school,
Mary Jo never shared anything.

She was too shy to tell the girls and boys
about anything.

She didn't think they would listen to her.

Miss Willet would say, "Mary Jo,
do you have something to share with us
this morning?"

Mary Jo always shook her head
and looked down at the floor.

"Why don't you ever share anything?"
her friend Laurie asked.

"I will some day," said Mary Jo.
"I just don't want to today."
Mary Jo really did want to share,
but she was too shy.

At night her father would ask,
"Did you share something today?"

"Not today," Mary Jo would say.

One morning it was raining.

When Mary Jo saw the rain, she thought,
"I'll share my new umbrella.

I can't wait to get to school."

Mary Jo ate her breakfast as fast·
as she could.

Then she put on her raincoat
and got out her new yellow umbrella.

This was her very first umbrella.

When Mary Jo got to school, she saw many other umbrellas!

"Everyone in school has an umbrella," thought Mary Jo.

"Maybe an umbrella isn't a good thing to share after all."

At Sharing Time, Miss Willet said, "Mary Jo, do you have something to share this morning?"

Mary Jo shook her head and looked down at the floor.

The next day Mary Jo and her brother
found a grasshopper.

They put it in a can.

The can had holes in the top of it.

"I'll share the grasshopper!"
thought Mary Jo.

So she took the grasshopper to school.

When Mary Jo got to school, she saw
the other children looking at something.

Mary Jo put her things away.
Then she went to see
what the other children were looking at.

"Jimmy's got three grasshoppers!"
said Laurie.
"He found them all by himself."

Mary Jo thought about the one grasshopper
her brother had helped her find.

"I don't think I'll share my grasshopper
after all," thought Mary Jo.

At Sharing Time, Miss Willet said,
"Mary Jo, do you have something to share
this morning?"

Mary Jo shook her head
and looked down at the floor.

All the other children
in Miss Willet's room shared things.

They shared their books.

They shared letters
from their grandmothers.

Sometimes they shared things
they found in the woods.

"What can I share?" Mary Jo asked herself
over and over.

She wanted to share something that no one
in her room had ever shared.

Mary Jo Thinks of Something

One night Mary Jo's father asked,
"Did you share something today, Mary Jo?"

Mary Jo said, "Not today."

Just then she thought of something!
"Could you go to school with me
in the morning?" she asked her father.

190

"In the morning?" asked her father.
"Why, yes, I think I can."

"Good!" said Mary Jo.
"Then you can come
and hear me share something."

"All right," said her father.
"What are you going to share?"

"It's a secret," said Mary Jo.

The next day, Mary Jo and her father
got to school early.

Miss Willet said she was very happy
Mary Jo's father had come to school.

"I've got something to share today,"
said Mary Jo.

"But it's a secret."

"I'm happy you have something
to share," Miss Willet said.

When it was Sharing Time, Miss Willet asked, "Who has something to share?"

Mary Jo put up her hand.
"I do," she said.
And she went to the front of the room.

"This morning I am going to share my father," Mary Jo said.

This made all the children smile.

Mary Jo's father smiled, too, and waited to be shared.

"This is my father," said Mary Jo.
"His name is Mr. William Wood.
He and my mother have three children.
I'm one of the children."

Jimmy put up his hand.
"My father grew up in the West,"
said Jimmy.
"Where did your father come from?"

"My father came from the West, too,"
said Mary Jo.

"He is a teacher.
He likes to read.
And he likes to go fishing."

"So does my father!" said Pam.

"My father puts up houses," said Dan.

They all wanted to share their fathers!
"Children," said Miss Willet, "Mary Jo
is telling us about her father today."

"When my father was little," Mary Jo
went on, "he wasn't always good."

One of the children asked, "What did
he do?"

"Well, one day he ate all of the cake
his mother had made for a school dinner,"
Mary Jo said.

After Mary Jo had told about her father,
she said, "Now my father will talk to you."

Mr. Wood smiled and talked
about how much he liked coming
to Miss Willet's room.

Mary Jo felt good.
At last she had shared something
that no one in her room had thought
of sharing.

Hop-Along Grasshopper

There are many kinds of grasshoppers.
Some grasshoppers live in the grass.
Some grasshoppers live in trees.

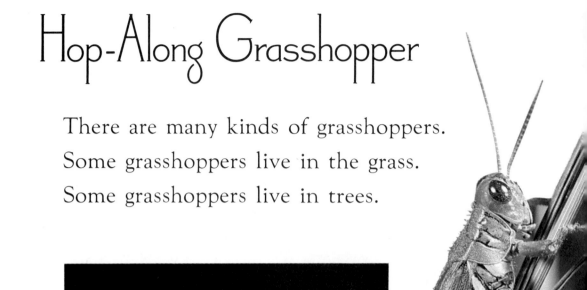

Most grasshoppers live where there is
grass to eat.

And all grasshoppers hop.

Grasshopper is a good name for something
that hops in the grass.

Not all grasshoppers have the same colors.
What colors do you see
in these grasshoppers?

Grasshoppers walk.

Grasshoppers fly.

But most of the time, grasshoppers
hop and jump.

Grasshoppers are very good jumpers.

A grasshopper takes jumps
that are much longer than
the grasshopper itself.

Grasshoppers have two big eyes
and three little eyes.

With all those eyes, grasshoppers see
very well.

They can see everything that moves.

If anything looks scary to a grasshopper,
the grasshopper has time to jump away.

Grasshoppers may be little, but they
can take care of themselves.

Jumping well and seeing well are
two ways grasshoppers have of taking care
of themselves.

MOON MOUSE

by ADELAIDE HOLL

One night Mother Mouse called,
"Come, Arthur.

Now that you are older,
you may stay up after dark.

Let us look at the night sky."

Arthur ran to the door and looked out.
Darkness was everywhere.
The night was very still.

"So this is what the night is like!
It is wonderful!" he said.

Arthur looked up.
There in the darkness was something
                    big
                        and round
                            and yellow.
"Look! What is that?" he asked.

"It is just the moon," his mother said.
"It is the big, round, yellow moon."

"Where is the moon?" asked Arthur.

"Very far away," his mother said.
"Way up in the sky."

"What is the moon for?" asked Arthur.

Mother Mouse said, "It lights up the sky
at night."

"What is it made of?" asked Arthur.

"I do not know," said his mother.
"I have heard that it is made of cheese.
But I do not think so."

"I would like to go to the moon,"
said Arthur.

His mother smiled.
"Not tonight," she said.
"Come. It is bedtime."

Arthur thought about the moon.
He thought about it day after day.
He thought about it night after night.

"How far away is the moon?" he asked
his mother one day.

"Very, very far away," she told him.

One night, Arthur said to himself,
"I am old enough to stay up after dark.
I must be old enough to go to the moon."

He looked up.
The sky was dark.
He could not see
the round, yellow moon anywhere.
"I will go and look for the moon,"
said Arthur to himself.

So away he went.

He went a long way,

a very long way.

He went a very, very long way.

Arthur went on and on until he came
to a place with many houses.

And there he saw the moon
sitting at the very top of a house.

He saw steps going up and up and up.

"This must be the way to the moon,"
he thought.

Up, up the steps he went.

At the top, he saw an open place.

"This must be the door to the moon,"
he said to himself.

And he went in.

Sure enough!
Inside was something
      big
         and round
            and yellow.
And it was made of cheese!

"It is the moon!" said Arthur.

He ran all around the big cheese.

He ran in and out of the little holes.

He ate some of the cheese.

He ate a little here and a little there.

At last, he was very full and very sleepy.

"The moon is a wonderful place,"
he said to himself.

"But I think I will go home now."

He went back
        down
            the
                steps.
And away he went.

He went a long way,

a very long way,

a very, very long way.

He went all the way home.

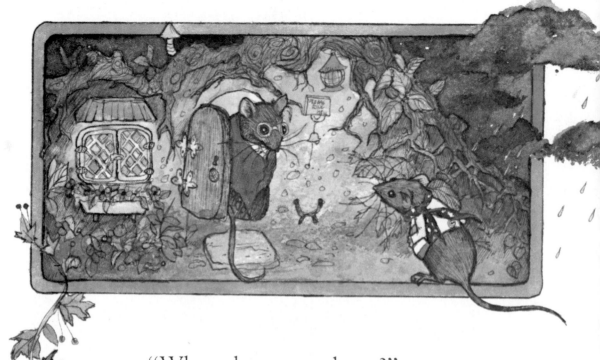

"Where have you been?"
asked Mother Mouse.
"I have been looking for you."

"I have been all the way to the moon,"
said Arthur.
"It *is* big and round and yellow.
It *is* made of cheese.
And it is very good."

Mother Mouse smiled.
"Funny little mouse!" she said.

Arthur looked up at the night sky.
It was raining.
And it was very dark.

"Where is the moon?" he asked
his mother.

"It is a rainy night," she said.
"The moon is hiding."

Arthur looked for the moon
the next night, and the next.
Night after night he waited.
But there was just the darkness
and the rain.

Then one night, the rain stopped.
The moon came out.
It was yellow.
But it was not big and round.
Arthur could see
just a little of the moon.
One side of the moon was not there.

"Look!" Arthur called to his mother.
"See how much of the moon I ate!"

His mother just laughed.
"It is a good thing you did not eat it
all up!" she said.

In the Dark of Night

by AILEEN FISHER

A mouse goes out
in the dark of night
without a lantern
or other light.
She's not afraid
of the dark at all,
though the night's so big
and herself so small.

Books to Enjoy

Hey, Kid! by Rita Golden Gelman
   Find out how a funny surprise
gets to be a big problem.

Little Chick's Story by Mary D. Kwitz
   Little Chick listens to a story
about herself.

Trouble Is His Name
by Elizabeth Rider Montgomery
   Jack gets a monkey — and then
some monkey problems, too!

Double Dog Dare by Ray Prather
   Find out how a girl helps two boys
come down from a tree.

Curious George Flies a Kite by Margret Rey
   George the monkey gets into trouble
when he tries to fish and to fly a kite.

Credits

Sounds You Know

b c d f g h j k l m n p r s t w v x y

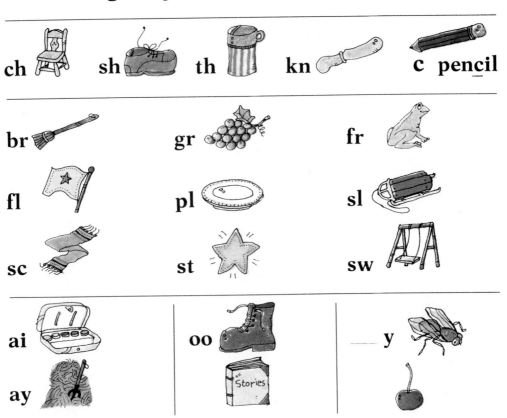

ch   sh   th   kn   **c** pen_cil

br   gr   fr

fl   pl   sl

sc   st   sw

ai   oo   ___ y

ay

New Sounds

cr   dr   pr   cl   sm

qu   squ   z   wr

Turn the page.

More Sounds You Know

short **a** sound

    can   am   hat

long **a** sound

    make   sale   game

short **e** sound

    get   red   them

long **e** sound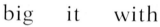

    be   tree   feet

short **i** sound

    big   it   with

long **i** sound

    like   time   ride

More New Sounds

short **o** sound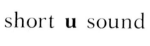

    stop   got   not

long **o** sound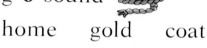

    home   gold   coat

short **u** sound

    cut   run   up

long **u** sound

    use

When you come to a new word —

    Read to the end of the sentence.

    Think about what the words are saying.

    Think about the sounds for letters.